Quality Assurance Monitoring in Occupational Therapy

Barbara E. Joe, MA
Patricia C. Ostrow, MA, OTR, FAOTA

The American Occupational Therapy Association, Inc.
Rockville, Maryland

The American Occupational Therapy Association, Inc.
1383 Piccard Drive
Rockville, MD 20850

Published 1987
Printed in the United States of America

Library of Congress Cataloging in Publication Data for this publication will be added when it is reprinted.

Cover Design by Robert Sacheli
Editing, text design, and composition by Edelfelt Johnson, Chapel Hill, North Carolina

Contents

About the Authors

Barbara E. Joe, MA, is Quality Assurance and Program Evaluation Specialist in the Quality Assurance Division of the American Occupational Therapy Association. She has written extensively on quality assurance and has given a number of lectures for both local and national audiences. Ms. Joe also answers direct inquiries on quality assurance from Association members and coordinates a national network of volunteer consultants who serve members in their region with quality assurance information especially tailored to their needs.

Patricia C. Ostrow, MA, OTR, FAOTA, is Director of the Quality Assurance Division of the American Occupational Therapy Association. Her writings, lectures, and demonstration projects on quality assurance have reached a wide audience in the United States and abroad. Ms. Ostrow has been a pioneer in disseminating efficacy data about occupational therapy and in streamlining techniques for data gathering for patient care evaluation to improve occupational therapy services and promote the profession.

Acknowledgments

Development of this manual grew out of requests for information from members of the American Occupational Therapy Association all across the nation. We are grateful for their questions and inspiration, which guided us throughout the preparation process. Special mention is due Margo Johnson for her editing services and Sandra Lee for typing the manuscript and preparing the charts. Thanks go also to Sara Brayman and Marvin Christianson, who reviewed an early draft and offered comments and suggestions.

Barbara E. Joe, MA
Patricia C. Ostrow, MA, OTR, FAOTA

1 Introduction

Quality assurance is not a brand new enterprise, but has historic roots. E. A. Codman, MD, writing over 70 years ago, pointed out that "hospitals, if they wish to be sure of improvement, must find out what their results are. Must analyze their results, to find their strong and weak points. Must compare their results with those of other hospitals" (as quoted by Greeley & Associates, 1983, p. 16.) In 1919, the American College of Surgeons established hospital standards, and in 1948, the Joint Commission on Accreditation of Hospitals (JCAH) was formed. From those beginnings the current systems of quality assurance emerged.

Quality assurance is not just the responsibility of management or administration. "Quality and service . . . To get them, of course, everyone's cooperation is required, not just mighty labors from the top 200" (Peters & Waterman, 1982, p. xxii).

Monitoring is the basic step in quality assurance currently required by the JCAH. The idea of monitoring is continuous evaluation, not a start-and-stop process. Through its requirements of regular measurement, analysis, and reporting of data on patient outcomes (and costs), monitoring is useful not only for meeting accreditation requirements, but for heightening the impact of care, promoting programs, and improving reimbursement. Monitoring also reveals problems and shows when they have been solved. The kind of outcomes assessment derived from quality assurance monitoring can be tied into the program evaluation system required by the Commission on Accreditation of Rehabilitation Facilities. It can also be a powerful tool to describe the impact of occupational therapy services to legislators, consumers, and other health care practitioners.

The basic areas monitored are called indicators—that is, indicators of quality health services. These relate to overall treatment goals and reflect important aspects of patient care. Measurable goals are set by staff for the expected patient care outcomes to be achieved, and percentage standards are established for the frequency of occurrence. If the data show that a program meets or exceeds standards, if effectiveness and efficiency can thereby be demonstrated, monitoring can become an important instrument for promoting services and improving occupational therapy utilization and reimbursement. Indicators and standards are discussed at greater length later on.

The purpose of this manual is to increase understanding of quality assurance monitoring and to offer guides and examples for the development of indicators for particular clinical settings. The manual offers the basic building blocks of a system that meets JCAH requirements and has been field-tested by occupational therapists who are experts in quality assurance, the volunteer Quality Assurance Consultants of the American Occupational Therapy Association (AOTA). The examples used, specific to occupational therapy, do not come directly from the JCAH. Furthermore, the examples and model offered here—stressing treatment goals and patient outcomes— provide only one way of meeting JCAH quality-assurance standards.

References

Greeley & Associates. (1983). *Continuous monitoring and data-based quality assurance* (Vol. 1). Salem, WI: Author.

Peters, T. J., & Waterman, R. H. (1982). *In search of excellence.* New York: Harper & Row.

2 Requirements of the Joint Commission on Accreditation of Hospitals

According to *Webster's* (1986), the verb *to monitor* means "to watch, observe, or check especially for a special purpose" (p. 767). Monitoring means measuring what a health care service is achieving and reporting on it at regular intervals. If achievement is less than expected, remedial action is called for. This chapter looks at quality assurance primarily from the standpoint of the JCAH, but it offers examples from the experience of practicing occupational therapists. The operational system developed out of the quality assurance experience of these therapists is more fully described in Chapter 6. One focus of this chapter is the specialized quality-assurance vocabulary of the JCAH that needs to be understood and mastered.

Standard 19.4.1 in the Rehabilitation Section of the JCAH *Accreditation Manual for Hospitals/86* describes quality assurance as "a planned and systematic process for the monitoring and evaluation of the quality and appropriateness of patient care, and for resolving identified problems" (JCAH, 1985, p. 234). Quality assurance is an evaluation system that helps an occupational therapy service answer questions such as How will our department know if we are providing quality care? What do we expect patients to accomplish as a result of occupational therapy? How can we demonstrate the impact of treatment?

The current monitoring had its beginnings in the 1979 JCAH quality assurance changes but was not formally described until 1982, when a quality assurance program was required to be "an ongoing planned and systematic process for monitoring and evaluating patient care" (JCAH, 1984, p. 8) Since then, the system has undergone additional evolution and refinement and doubtless will continue to be modified over time.

JCAH surveys are regularly scheduled every three years, and they place greatest emphasis on the year just preceding their occurrence. Failure to have a quality-assurance monitoring system in place will result in a contingency that must be corrected at six months' follow-up if accreditation is to remain in force. There is no requirement that quality assurance activities be disclosed to the public, and quality assurance meetings are confidential. However, quality assurance material may be used for staff educational purposes, according to the

JCAH (Quality Assurance in Support Services seminar, July 10-11, 1986, Orlando, FL).

To effectively evaluate and monitor the quality and the appropriateness of patient care, occupational therapy staff need to establish specific criteria for the care of each group of patients. These criteria become yardsticks for quality. The JCAH does not further specify the characteristics of criteria. However, the agency does stress the need for "objective criteria that reflect current knowledge and clinical experience" (JCAH, 1985, p. 265). For example, one criterion of patient satisfaction with occupational therapy treatment would be patients answering yes to the discharge question, Were you satisfied with your care? In addition, especially in rehabilitation, percentage standards of compliance with criteria are often set. In the example just given, a related standard might be the expectation that 80% of patients would be satisfied with their treatment.[1] Both criteria and standards are determined by reference to research and/or the consensus of professionals with knowledge of the area being measured (Donabedian, 1986, p. 105; Williamson, Ostrow, & Braswell, 1981, pp. 32-40).

Criteria and standards based on outcomes achieved under experimental conditions often must be adapted to a nonexperimental setting, and exact replication of results cannot be expected. In some cases, rather than being an exact model, research becomes a reference and a take-off point for the development of standards in a given clinical setting. (See Donabedian, 1986, for a further discussion of quality assurance criteria and standards.)

When the care provided by the professionals in a particular clinical setting does not comply with criteria and standards developed by those professionals, this signifies a problem or an opportunity for improvement, and corrective action is required. After such action has been taken, the monitoring system will show whether the standard has been achieved and the problem corrected.

Criteria and standards are the building blocks of more general indicators (sometimes also called monitors). According to the JCAH *1986 Generic Model for Monitoring and Evaluation,* indicators show whether

[1] The JCAH does not require the establishment of percentage standards along with criteria, but AOTA's Quality Assurance Division recommends their use as a way to judge whether results are satisfactory.

patient care was *appropriately* delivered and was of *high quality*. Indicators should be related to goals and other aspects of care that have a meaningful impact on patients' lives, meaningful not only to therapists, but also to patients subjectively. In the example given earlier, patient satisfaction would be the indicator. The JCAH (1986) defines an indicator as "a measurable component of patient/resident care that is indicative of either high- or low-quality care" (*1986 Generic Model of Monitoring and Evaluation,* p. 1).

The JCAH (1986) further defines monitoring as the "systematic and routine process of gathering important clinical data and aggregating or displaying data so that problems or opportunities to improve care can be identified" (*1986 Generic Model of Monitoring and Evaluation,* p. 1). If possible, monitoring should be tied to existing data sources and data collection efforts.

Possible data sources include the following:

- Direct observation
- Patients' charts
- Incident reports
- Safety checklists
- Surveys of patients or families
- Patients' complaints
- Surveys of staff
- Missed treatments
- Initial, discharge, and follow-up assessments
- Cost and volume statistics (as they represent the cost-effectiveness aspect of quality care).

The experience of occupational therapists performing quality assurance indicates that to facilitate monitoring, it is advisable to set up a patient records system that collects and registers measurable data routinely in the course of treatment.

Table 1 lists sample rehabilitation criteria developed by a JCAH survey team. It suggests that each major function be reviewed for quality.

References

Donabedian, A. (1986, March). Criteria and standards for quality assessment and monitoring. *Quarterly Review Bulletin* (Joint Commission on Accreditation of Hospitals), pp. 99-105.

Joint Commission on Accreditation of Hospitals. (1984). *Quality assurance in support services.* Chicago: Author.

Joint Commission on Accreditation of Hospitals. (1985). *Accreditation manual for hospitals/86.* Chicago: Author.

Joint Commission on Accreditation of Hospitals. (1986). *1986 generic model of monitoring and evaluation.* Chicago: Author.

Webster's ninth new collegiate dictionary. (1986). Springfield, MA: Merriam-Webster.

Williamson, J. W., Ostrow, P. C., & Braswell, H. R. (1981). *Health accounting for quality assurance: A manual for assessing and improving outcomes of care.* Rockville, MD: American Occupational Therapy Association.

Table 1. Sample Rehabilitation Criteria Developed by a JCAH Survey Team

Function A—Evaluation/Assessment of Patients' Needs

Indicator 1—Initial Intake Evaluation/Assessment of Patients' Needs
Criteria: 1. Initial assessment performed within 2 days of admission by therapist and physician director
2. Duration of treatment established through consultation of therapist and attending physician

Indicator 2—Appropriateness of Evaluation
Criteria: 1. All elements addressed by evaluation, per diagnosis and per established departmental criteria
2. Realistic goals established for diagnostic condition
3. Proper therapeutic modality/modalities recommended for diagnostic condition

Indicator 3—Timeliness of Therapy Initiation
Criterion: 1. No more than 24 hours time elapsed between MD order and initial treatment

Function B—Development of Treatment Plans and Goals

Indicator 1—Patient's Response to Established Treatment Plan
Criterion: 1. Reevaluation of patients physical/mental status by discipline or multidisciplinary team within 3 days

Indicator 2—Family's Response to Established Treatment Plan
Criterion: 1. Evidence of family acceptance and cooperation with treatment plans/goals

Indicator 3—Availability of Therapy Services Indicated by Treatment Plan
Criterion: 1. Priorities of treatment provided for in patient assessment

Function C—Application and Assessment of Therapies Used

Indicator 1—Adequacy of Duration of Therapy
Criterion: 1. Goals achieved within therapy time established

Indicator 2—Number of Missed Therapy Sessions
Criterion: 1. No missed sessions except for medical complications

Indicator 3—Adjustments/Modifications of Therapy Treatment
Criterion: 1. Complications from treatment identified and treatment plan adjusted accordingly

Function D—Patient/Family Counseling

Indicator 1—Patient/Family Understanding of Therapy Exercises
Criteria: 1. Required exercises demonstrated by patient/family without any assistance from staff
2. Number of postdischarge calls for assistance

Indicator 2—Appropriateness of Counseling Activities
Criterion: 1. Where indicated, family involved in treatment planning at time of initial evaluation

Indicator 3—Readmission of Patients for Additional Therapy
Criterion: 1. No revisits or readmissions of patients for additional therapy within a specified time frame

Note: This list is an educational sample only. It is not intended to be complete or suitable for all facilities.

3 Steps in Monitoring

The monitoring system recommended here follows a quality-assurance problem-solving process of five basic steps. Williamson, Ostrow, and Braswell (1981) describe the steps in a quality assurance study in full detail as applied to the discovery and resolution of problems in health care delivery. With a slight shift in Stage 1, their work is applicable to monitoring.

First, indicators of important aspects of patient care are identified and criteria established, based on the literature and/or professional consensus. In addition, the caregivers set standards of compliance in terms of the percentage of cases that they expect to meet each criterion.

Second, data are collected, analyzed, and evaluated. If outcomes meet or exceed standards, this validates current performance and may be useful in program promotion. If outcomes fall short of standards, remedial action is called for, and Step 3 is taken.

Third, the cause of the problem is assessed and a plan for improvement action developed. Many problems can be easily remedied; others require large-scale action. Whichever is the case, the following must be designated:

- *Who* is responsible?
- *What* actions are to be taken?
- *When*?

It is best, if possible, to keep time frames short and actions simple.

Next, the remedial action is implemented. This obviously important component of health care problem-solving is sometimes neglected.

Finally, to determine if the problem has been solved, data are again collected, analyzed, and evaluated according to the standard. This last step is very important. If the problem remains unsolved, the caregivers should go back to the third step, improvement planning. If the problem has been solved, periodic monitoring will show whether it remains in control. Table 2 outlines the steps in quality assurance monitoring.

Reference

Williamson, J. W., Ostrow, P. C., & Braswell, H. R. (1981). *Health accounting for quality assurance: A manual for assessing and improving outcomes of care.* Rockville, MD: American Occupational Therapy Association.

Table 2. Steps in Quality Assurance Monitoring

1. Identify overall indicators of quality care.
   Select measures/criteria; set standards.
   What will you see if quality care is occurring?

2. Collect data.
   Decide what, where, how, and when to measure selected indicator.
   If standards are being met, report this.
   If not, go to Step 3.

3. Determine cause of problem and formulate plan for remedial action.

4. Implement remedial action.

5. Measure again to see if problem has been solved.
   If so, repeat measures periodically to ensure that quality standards are maintained.
   If not, go back to Step 3.

4 Selecting and Developing Indicators and Criteria

In choosing indicators of quality care, it is necessary to relate them to the overall goals of the occupational therapy department and the facility, such as assisting patients to live independently, live in the community, be productive citizens, and be able to function adequately in activities of daily living (ADL). These goals need to be more precisely defined and described, then broken down into concrete, measurable objectives or criteria. For example, for mental health patients, being a productive citizen might be defined as improved patient productivity. This would be measured by specific criteria, such as a given number of hours per week spent fulfilling appropriate roles, producing useful items, and/or providing service to others with or without remuneration.

All professional staff should be involved in choosing indicators and criteria. The JCAH makes it clear that front-line therapists and assistants alike should understand why quality assurance data are being collected and how they will be used (Quality Assurance in Support Services seminar, July 10-11, 1986, Orlando, FL). Also, to the extent possible, patients should be involved, in making suggestions about what characterizes quality care and in assessing the quality of care via interviews or questionnaires. Contract services are not exempt from quality assurance and must be evaluated by the agency performing the services, although the hospital contracting for the services has oversight responsibility too.

Quality assurance indicators and the specific criteria used to measure them should build on data already available or being collected, when possible. Criteria should be kept simple. Regular patient documentation should be designed to collect data relevant to quality assurance in numerical form in the course of treatment, if that is not already the case. Because patient outcomes are important for both individual treatment and quality assurance monitoring, essentially the same data can be used for both. The difference is that for quality assurance purposes, data on individual patients are clustered to reveal patterns of outcomes for groups.

Not all data documenting the care of individual patients need to be aggregated for quality assurance, however. In the model offered here, quality assurance is concerned primarily with data reporting treatment outcomes. Quality assurance problems show systematic patterns; that is, monitoring picks up and deals with repeated problems in the same area. A one-time event is not a quality assurance problem unless it reflects a dire and dangerous situation.

In choosing indicators, each department should start with the most important ones, usually 5-10, and add others over time. Indicators should be chosen that are in high-risk, problem-prone activities and that also demonstrate the quality of care. It is advisable to have at least some indicators that include cost data.

All indicators must reflect important aspects of patient care and outcomes. If monitoring shows standards are being consistently met, measuring and reporting intervals may be lengthened. If after six months no problem surfaces on an indicator, data collection efforts for it may be dropped and something else substituted (JCAH, Quality Assurance in Support Services seminar, July 10-11, 1986, Orlando, FL).

To get a better fix on patterns, the JCAH advises taking consecutive rather than random samples. Concurrent review is recommended because retrospective review may not give a good picture of current care and may let problems run too long before being corrected. One of the purposes of monitoring is to catch problems in the beginning stages. If no problems appear over long periods, the monitoring system is inadequate, according to the JCAH (Quality Assurance in Support Services seminar, July 10-11, 1986, Orlando, FL).

Although the JCAH definitely favors monitoring all patients in a given diagnostic category where feasible, exceptions are possible. As long as a patient sample can be justified as representative, sampling is permissible. Also, all patients do not have to be measured continuously; for example, measures could be taken for two weeks, stopped, and repeated for two weeks in the next quarter.

The JCAH previously mandated reporting on a quarterly basis. The agency still requires reporting, but it no longer specifies the interval. That is, reporting may be monthly, quarterly, annually—whatever is appropriate for a particular indicator. A common pattern is for departments to gather data monthly and report quarterly.

Some warnings about generalizations: First, until confirmed by subsequent monitoring, initial monitoring results should be viewed with neither alarm nor complacency. In other words, strong conclusions—good or bad—should not be drawn from first results, which may be atypical. The idea of continuous monitoring is precisely to discover patterns over time.

Second, transferring standards from one setting to another should be done cautiously. Although standards are based on professional consensus and the literature and therefore may have some generalizability, the results are applicable only to the setting in which they were measured. Specific indicators must always be adapted to a particular practice setting.

Table 3 summarizes some monitoring do's and don't's.

Table 3. Monitoring Do's and Don't's

1. Do relate indicators to organizational purpose, e.g., improving the patient's ability to live independently.
2. Do involve staff in choosing indicators.
3. Do build on data already being collected.
4. Don't monitor everything; choose indicators demonstrating quality care.
5. Do include cost data.
6. Don't necessarily take a quality assurance study and make it continuing.
7. Do base standards on professional consensus and/or research, not automatically on the current results of care.
8. Do report findings regularly, but not necessarily quarterly.
9. Do add new indicators as needed.
10. Do reduce frequency of monitoring as appropriate.
11. Don't draw hard conclusions from first results.
12. Do be cautious about comparing standards and results from different clinical settings.

5 Cost Considerations

Monitoring may be concerned with costs as well as with outcomes of patient care. Costs have always been a factor in judging quality. Donabedian's (1982) description of quality care includes both costs and health benefits: "The net benefit to health must exceed the monetary cost incurred in obtaining the benefit" (p. 5).

Formal calculation of net benefit requires attribution of some dollar value to the health component. For example, in addition to contributing to patient well-being, training in activities of daily living may prevent the need for costly nursing home placement or reduce the number of hours of paid assistance required by a patient returning home. Quality assurance sometimes can circumvent the need to establish a monetary benefit for patient outcomes by demonstrating cost-effectiveness through alternative means, by either (a) reducing current costs with no decrease in patient benefits or (b) keeping costs constant and increasing patient benefits. Thus, cost-effectiveness is established without having to put a dollar value on patient benefits.

A midwestern rehabilitation service, for example, was able to decrease its cost per successful case by 26.5% while holding overall occupational therapy costs constant. Successful cases were defined as those in which patients had improved one or more levels in at least one area of self-care at discharge and had maintained the discharge level at 60-day follow-up. Before initiating improvement action, the service tallied 57 successful cases, 26 unsuccessful ones. After improvement, there were 73 successful cases and 8 unsuccessful ones. Cost savings per successful case in one quarter were calculated at $1,482.79 (Christianson, 1984).

Although JCAH quality assurance requirements do not currently specify collection of cost data, nevertheless, criteria for appropriate utilization of care may have cost implications, and JCAH's timetable calls for an increasing emphasis on appropriateness criteria starting in 1987. Appropriateness usually refers to the level of care provided: Does it coincide with the patient's needs, neither more nor less than the patient requires? Appropriate utilization has implications for cost benefits as well as patient benefits.

In the area of appropriateness, the emphasis of the JCAH, and of the governmental watchdogs called Peer

Review Organizations (PROs), seems mainly on the elimination of unnecessary care or of care beyond the level actually required. This is an area in which quality assurance can contribute to cost-effectiveness.

The following example from a mental health setting shows how quality assurance monitoring helped solve a problem with cost implications by reducing the time therapists spent waiting for patients who did not keep their appointments. In this case, quality assurance monitoring in an acute-care psychiatric occupational therapy program indicated an excessive number of patient no-shows resulting in missed occupational therapy appointments. Several staff and patient education measures were introduced, but monitoring indicated that the number of missed appointments still remained at unacceptably high levels, based on preestablished standards.

A closer analysis of the data revealed that a small number of patients who never kept their occupational therapy appointments were responsible for the bulk of no-shows. When a concerted effort to have these patients participate in the occupational therapy treatment program failed, they were terminated from occupational therapy services. New criteria for appropriateness of utilization were established for occupational therapy, according to which a psychiatric patient who missed two consecutive weeks of treatment appointments without good cause and in spite of concerted efforts by staff was considered currently ineligible for occupational therapy services and automatically terminated. The patient was informed that occupational therapy could resume when he or she made a commitment to be present at scheduled sessions. When this policy was implemented, the number of missed appointments fell within the standard, and therapists were able to devote their time to patients who reliably attended scheduled appointments.

References

Christianson, M. (1984). *Cost analysis of a QA study.* Grand Falls, ND: Medical Center Rehabilitation Hospital.

Donabedian, A. (1982). *The criteria and standards of quality* (Vol. 2). Ann Arbor, MI: Health Administration Press.

6 Examples of Quality Assurance Indicators and Monitoring Reports

Once the rationale for the general process of quality assurance monitoring is understood, this understanding can best be expanded by looking at specific examples of quality indicators and at sample formats for reporting quality-assurance monitoring activities. A number of these appear in this chapter, beginning with Table 4, which gives some examples of quality assurance indicators, along with possible ways that quality could be measured for them.

A more detailed example may serve to illustrate the actual process of formulating quality assurance indicators. A hypothetical occupational therapy department has a goal of enabling stroke patients to return home. Staff have defined ability to return home as consisting of the following:

1. Transferring in and out of bed and chair
2. Dressing in a manner consistent with warmth and safety
3. Achieving mobility within the home
4. Attending to toilet needs and washing hands
5. Preparing hot drink and simple meal
6. Feeding self
7. Controlling light, heat, switches, locks, etc.

This example, which is adapted from a research study involving stroke patients (Garraway, Akhtar, Prescott, & Hockey, 1980; Smith, Garraway, Akhtar, & Andrews, 1977; Smith, Garraway, Smith, & Akhtar, 1982), does not include outdoor mobility, bathing, or shopping among the activities necessary to live independently in the home. Presumably, these latter needs can be met by friends, relatives, or home health service personnel on an occasional basis. However, all seven of the basic daily-living tasks mentioned must be demonstrated by the patient before he or she is considered able to be discharged home.

In addition to criteria, standards are set to indicate expected rates of achievement. Although 100% achievement is an ideal to strive for, reference to research or professional consensus may indicate that a compliance rate of less than 100% is acceptable, especially when the special characteristics of patients in a given setting are considered. Nevertheless, even when standards are set at less than 100%, all cases of nonachievement should be reviewed.

To determine a patient's ability to perform the seven tasks cited above, the therapist observes the patient's performance. The standard set—based on the literature, experts, and the experience of the occupational therapy department—is that 60% of stroke patients deemed to have rehabilitation potential should be able to perform the seven tasks after 12 consecutive occupational therapy treatments.

The occupational therapy department has a documentation system in place that routinely tabulates this type of information. After collecting and analyzing the data, the department finds that only 30% of its stroke patients are able to function in the seven areas after the specified number of treatments. Changes are initiated to increase this percentage, such as more active practice of daily-living skills on the ward and discussions with patients.

After implementation of these changes, data are collected again, and it is found that 50% of stroke patients are now able to perform the seven daily-living tasks after 12 treatments. This is an improvement, indicating that the action is moving in the right direction. Improvement efforts continue until the standard is reached or exceeded. Then they are incorporated permanently into the treatment program. Figure 1 shows how the monitoring results in this example might be displayed on a graph.

If outcomes come close to standards without quite reaching them, this may also be acceptable. In some cases, the standard may have been set too high or too low at the outset and have to be modified, though this should be a rare occurrence if due care is taken in setting the standard.

Some occupational therapy departments use existing treatment outcomes as their standards, finding a problem only when there is a marked deviation. If current treatment and its outcomes are considered the best that can be achieved with available resources, it is justifiable to use them as the basis of standards. However, this should be done cautiously, for such a policy tends to keep patient care at the status quo.

Additional samples of indicators and methods to document monitoring activities for the JCAH are shown in the following tables. These samples are illustrative only and may need to be adapted to a particular setting and patient mix.

In using the forms, the reader should keep in mind that criteria are the specific items measured that demonstrate achievement of indicators. There may be several measures or criteria relating to a particular indicator. For example, appropriate patient assessment may be an occupational therapy indicator. Criteria then show what needs to be measured and what the measurement should show in order to constitute an appropriate assessment.

The following tables provide examples of reporting formats and the type of information required for quality assurance monitoring. Table 5-a gives examples of indicators for occupational therapy in physical disabilities, and Table 6-a shows indicators in mental health. Criteria (measures for individual patients) as well as standards (percentage of achievement of criteria by groups of patients) are shown in the righthand column. These are based on professional consensus, research findings, and local conditions and therefore may vary somewhat. Standards, because of the many human factors involved, are usually not set at 100%.

Tables 5-b and 6-b, which accompany those just mentioned, are examples of monitoring summary reports, based generally on the five-step problem-solving system discussed earlier. Other reporting formats are possible that include even more detail, such as who is to collect what data and when. The specific reporting format is not as important as having one that shows essential information simply and clearly.

Tables 7-a, 7-b, 7-c, 7-d, and 8 illustrate another reporting format. Tables 7-a, 7-b, 7-c, and 7-d are a set. The measures reported in Table 7-a are based on the Barthel Index, which is summarized in Table 7-b. Table 7-c presents functional data for one hypothetical patient. Table 7-d contains the raw monitoring data summarized in columns 1, 6, and 12 of Table 7-a. Table 8 is another example of the monitoring summary in Table 7-a.

Materials to supplement this manual include the basic texts on quality-assurance skills, *Health Accounting for Quality Assurance: A Manual for Assessing and Improving Outcomes of Care* (1981) by Williamson, Ostrow, and Braswell, and *Quality Assurance Primer: Improving Health Care Outcomes and Productivity* (1983) by Ostrow, Williamson, and Joe. Also, *Occupational Therapy Documentation: A System to Capture Outcome*

Data for Quality Assurance and Program Promotion, by Kuntavanish (1987), provides a system for documenting, collecting, and reporting quality assurance data. Further questions about quality assurance monitoring may be directed to the AOTA's Quality Assurance Division.

References

Garraway, W. M., Akhtar, A. J., Prescott, R. J., & Hockey, L. (1980, April). Management of acute stroke in the elderly: Preliminary results of a controlled trial. *British Medical Journal,* pp. 1040-1043.

Kuntavanish, A. (1987). *Occupational therapy documentation: A system to capture outcome data for quality assurance and program promotion.* Rockville, MD: American Occupational Therapy Association.

Ostrow, P. C., Williamson, J. W., & Joe, B. E. (1983). *Quality assurance primer: Improving health care outcomes and productivity.* Rockville, MD: American Occupational Therapy Association.

Smith, M. E., Garraway, W. M., Akhtar, A. J., & Andrews, C. J. A. (1977, March). Measuring the outcome of stroke rehabilitation. *Occupational Therapy,* pp. 51-53.

Smith, M. E., Garraway, W. M., Smith, D. L., & Akhtar, A. J. (1982, January). Therapy impact on functional outcome in a controlled trial of stroke rehabilitation. *Archives of Physical Medicine and Rehabilitation, 63,* 21-24.

Williamson, J. W., Ostrow, P. C., & Braswell, H. R. (1981). *Health accounting for quality assurance: A manual for assessing and improving outcomes of care.* Rockville, MD: American Occupational Therapy Association.

Figure 1. Percentage of Stroke Patients Able to Function in Seven Designated Areas of Self-Care After 12 Occupational Therapy Treatments

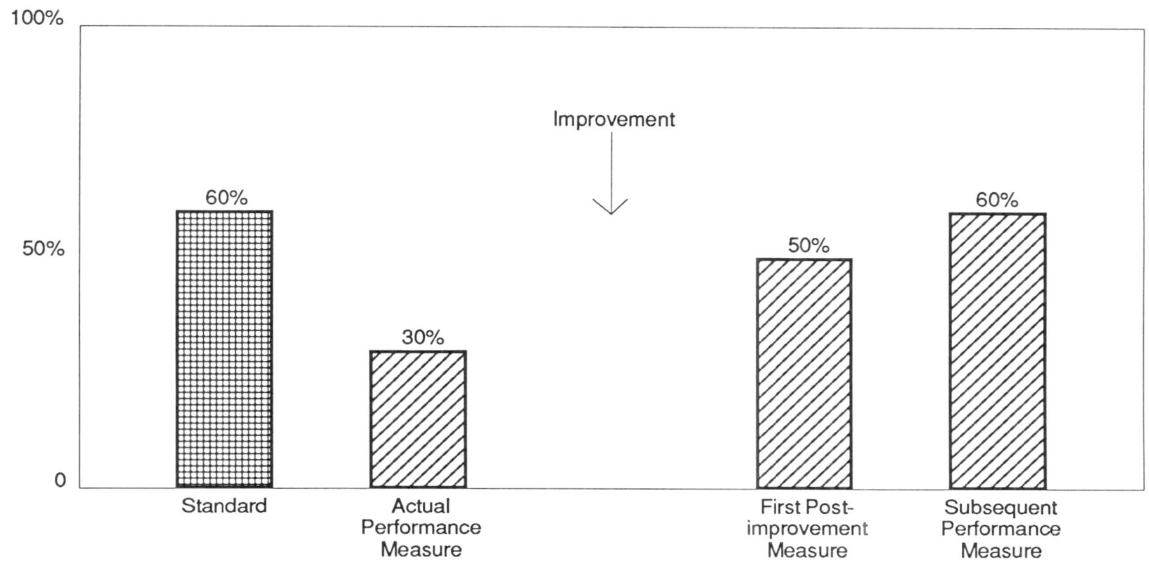

Table 4. Examples of Occupational Therapy Indicators

Indicator	General Measure
Responses to referrals are timely.	Responses within a specified period after referrals
Referrals are appropriate.	Referrals in line with referral criteria
Treatment plans are appropriate.	Protocols followed
Patients help establish their individual treatment goals.	Patients' participation documented
Missed therapy sessions are infrequent.	Fewer than a specified percentage within a given time frame
Accidents are reduced.	Fewer than a given number per month
Patients' functional status is improved.	Results of standardized test administered over time
Patients are satisfied with treatment outcomes.	Responses to survey of patients
Families are satisfied with their role in planning and goal setting.	Responses to survey of families
Cardiac patients' skill in stress management is increased.	Observations by therapist using checklist; physiological measures
Back patients' knowledge of back conservation is demonstrated.	Performance per checklist
Psychiatric patients' life-management skills are improved.	Scores on a selected psychiatric rating scale

Table 5-a. Quality-Assurance Monitoring Examples for Occupational Therapy Inpatients with Physical Disabilities

Occupational Therapy Monitoring Indicator	Measure	Applied to	Outcome Standard/Criteria[a]
Timely intake evaluation	Time between admission and evaluation	All patients	95% will have intake evaluation performed within two days of admission.
Establishment of mutual treatment goals with patients	Documentation in chart that patient has participated in goal selection Patients' rating of goal significance	All patients in rehabilitation	90% will have participated in setting goals, and 80% will have an overall rating of their goals as at least moderately significant.
Patient attendance at occupational therapy sessions	Documentation of therapy attendance	All acute care patients	97% will have no missed sessions except those caused by medical complications.
Increased level of self-care for acute care patients	Functional level before and after five consecutive treatments	Acute care patients with goal of improved function	85% will move up one functional level on ADL scale in one area of self-care.
Achievement of functional goals for head trauma patients	Barthel Index[b] at beginning and end of treatment	Head trauma patients	80% will achieve predicted goals by end of treatment.
Improvement in rehabilitation patients' ability to live independently at discharge	Total hours of ADL help per week patients would require, estimated at admission and discharge from occupational therapy by therapist and patient	All rehabilitation patients with loss of ADL skills and potential for discharge to home or minimal/moderate-care situation who receive minimum of five consecutive occupational therapy treatments	85% will decrease amount of ADL assistance needed by three or more hours per day.
Family member understanding of home therapy exercises	Family member demonstration of necessary exercises	Patients who have family member and need assistance with exercises after discharge	85% of family members (when understanding of patient exercises is indicated) will correctly demonstrate all necessary exercises before patient discharge.
Maintenance of average rehabilitation costs	Percentage of patient services at or below average rehabilitation costs	All physical disability patients in rehabilitation	70% of patients will be at or below average rehabilitation costs.

Note: The indicators are illustrative only; they do not represent the full range of treatments or types of patients served by occupational therapy. Likewise, the criteria and standards, though based on actual clinical examples, are illustrative only and not advocated or necessarily considered appropriate for all settings.

[a]All noncompliance with criteria will be reviewed to establish the reason why.

[b]From "Functional Evaluation: The Barthel Index," by F. I. Mahoney & D. W. Barthel, 1965, February, *Maryland State Medical Journal*, pp. 61-65.

Table 6-a. Quality-Assurance Monitoring Examples for Occupational Therapy Mental Health Inpatients

Occupational Therapy Monitoring Indicator	Measure	Applied to	Outcome Standard/Criteria
Prompt patient assessment	Time lag between occupational therapy referral and assessment	All psychiatric patients	90% of patients will be assessed within 24 hours of referral to occupational therapy.
Patient participation in goal-directed activities	Time per day spent in occupational therapy/ unit activities that have specific treatment goals	All patients in acute-care psychiatric unit	75% will spend three hours daily in goal-directed activity.
Increased independent functioning by patients	Mean difference between admission and discharge on Comprehensive Occupational Therapy Evaluation (COTE)[a] Scale	All psychiatric patients	80% of patients will decrease score by 10 or more points.
Improvement in successful placement in independent living	Scorable Self-Care Evaluation (SSCE)[b] administered before discharge	Psychiatric patients going into independent living	100% of patients will have overall score of 30 or less before being considered for independent living.

[a]From "Comprehensive Occupational Therapy Evaluation Scale" by S. J. Brayman, T. F. Kirby, A. M. Misenheimer, & M. J. Short, 1976, *American Journal of Occupational Therapy, 30,* 94-100.

[b]From *The Scorable Self-Care Evaluation (SSCE)* by N. Clark & M. Peters, 1984, Thorofare, NJ: Charles B. Slack.

Table 5-b. Sample Monitoring Summary Report

Indicator Number[a]	Data Location	Reviewer	Date	Results	Improvement Action, If Required
1	Intake records	Susan B. Clerk	9/1/86 9/8/86 9/15/86 9/22/86 9/29/86	100% 90% 100% 95% 100%	None
2	Patients' charts	Senior Therapist, OTR	9/30/86 10/31/86	40% 50%	1. Staff inservice on mutual goals 2. Doc. change to remind therapists to set mutual goals
3	Patients' charts	Susan B. Clerk	10/6/86 10/13/86 10/20/86 10/27/86	90% 95% 100% 100%	None
4	Rehab. data log	Senior Therapist, OTR	10/6/86 10/20/86	85% 90%	None
5	Rehab. data log	Senior Therapist, OTR	10/1/86 11/1/86 12/1/86	70% 80% 85%	None
6	Rehab. data log	Senior Therapist, OTR	9/1/86 10/1/86	50% 85%	See remarks
7	Rehab. data log	Fieldwork students	9/15/86	60%	More time teaching families; two practices before demonstration
8	Financial Records Department	Department head	10/1/86 11/1/86 12/1/86	75% 85% 70%	

Note: An actual monitoring report may reveal more areas for improvement action. This chart is illustrative only.

[a]Indicator number from Table 5-a

Table 6-b. Sample Monitoring Summary Report

Indicator Number[a]	Data Location	Reviewer	Date	Results	Improvement Action, If Required
1	Patients' charts	Susan B. Clerk	10/1/86 11/1/86 12/1/86	85% 100% 95%	None
2	Ward log	Susan B. Clerk	10/1/86 11/1/86 12/1/86	60% 65% 70%	See remarks
3	Patients' charts	Senior Therapist, OTR	10/1/86 11/1/86 12/1/86	80% 90% 85%	None
4	Patients' charts	Senior Therapist, OTR	10/1/86 11/1/86 12/1/86	85% 80% 85%	Therapist education as to what SSCE score signifies, importance of 30 or less score for successful independent placement

Note: An actual monitoring report may reveal more areas for improvement action. This chart is illustrative only.

[a]Indicator number from Table 6-a

Table 5-b (cont.)

Date Initiated	Reeval. Findings	Date	Quarterly Report to Whom	Date	Remarks
			Staff, QA Committee, Administrator	10/186	Review monthly.
11/15/86 12/1/86	80% 90%	12/31/86 1/1/87	Staff, QA Committee	1/2/87	Review again in 3 months.
			Staff, QA Committee	11/1/86	Review monthly.
			Staff, QA Committee	11/1/86	Reviewed first 30 charts only. Review in 3 months.
			Staff, QA Committee	11/1/86	Keep reviewing monthly for next quarter.
			Staff, QA Committee	11/1/86	First month, more ill patients. Keep reviewing monthly. May need better patient screening.
9/20/86	70% 75% 80%	10/15/86 11/15/86 12/15/86	Staff	1/2/87	Continue improvement action monthly until standard is met.

Table 6-b (cont.)

Date Initiated	Reeval. Findings	Date	Quarterly Report to Whom	Date	Remarks
			Staff, QA Committee, Administrator	1/2/87	Keep reviewing monthly.
			Staff, QA Committee, Administrator	1/2/87	Standard too high for current patient mix. Change to 65%. Continue reviewing monthly.
			Staff, QA Committee, Administrator	1/2/87	Increase standard to 85%.
12/7/86	90% 95%	12/15/86 12/30/86	Staff	1/2/87	Continue therapist education on SSCE. Counsel individual therapists who do not comply.

Table 7-a. Hypothetical Monitor No. 1

Date	Indicator Stage 1	Criteria/Standard/ Measure Stage 2	Location of Data	Reviewer/ Date	Results/Date	Date Reported to Staff and Dept.Chair
January–March 1986	Functional gain as measured by the Barthel Index, for up to the first 15 patients with a diagnosis of CVA or head trauma (see Tables 7-b, 7-c, and 7-d)	≥ 10 points of improvement at time of discharge 15% maximum acceptable nonachievement[a] Barthel score pre- and posttreatment, with a minimum of 5 consecutive treatments	Data log in Rehab. OT	A. B. & C. D. 3/29/86	13 Identified 9 Achieved standard 31% Nonachievement (NA) 3/29/86	4/4/86
April–June 1986	Same as above	Same as above	Same as above	A. B. & C. D. 6/28/86	14 Identified 11 Achieved standard 21% NA 6/28/86	7/4/86
July–September 1986	Same as above	Same as above	Same as above	A. B. & C. D. 9/27/86	10 Identified 10 Achieved standard 0% NA 9/27/86	10/3/86
October–December 1986	Same as above	Same as above	Same as above	A. B. & C. D. 12/27/86	15 Identified 14 Achieved standard 7% NA 12/27/86	1/9/87

Note: Adapted from forms developed by Anne A. Kuntavanish, OTR, FAOTA, Rehabilitation Services Administrator, Greater Southeast Community Hospital, Washington, DC. Reprinted by permission. The example draws on actual quality assurance activities but has been altered for reasons of confidentiality. The monitoring system illustrated is basd on the five-stage problem-solving process of quality assurance described in Chapter 3.

[a]Whereas the goal is theoretically 100%, the consensus of professional opinion for this hypothetical study is that 15% of the patients in this facility will be unable to achieve the outcomes for valid reasons. All incidents in which the criteria are not achieved will be reviewed.

Table 7-a (cont.)

Impact of Achieving Standard	Date	Recs. for Improvement Action Stage 3	Implem. Date & Improvement Action Stage 4	Reeval. Date/ Result Stage 5	Date Reported to Staff & Dept. Chair	Remarks
Maximum functional restoration Feedback on program effectiveness and efficiency as compared with the established standard	4/4/86	Monitor each patient's plan of care carefully.	4/8/86—Monitor each patient's plan of care carefully.	6/2/86 21% NA	Staff 7/4/86	Barthel Index is not refined enough for small increments of progress.
Same as above	7/4/86	Establish uniform grading guideline for staff in Barthel rating.	7/4/86—Continue to monitor this population. Establish uniform grading guideline for staff in Barthel rating.	9/27/86 0% NA	Staff 10/3/86	
Same as above	10/3/86	Continue to monitor functional outcomes.	10/3/86—Continue to monitor functional outcomes.	12/27/86 7% NA	Staff 1/9/87	Is 10-point increase on the Barthel significant?
Same as above	1/9/87	Conduct inservice with staff on Barthel rating.				

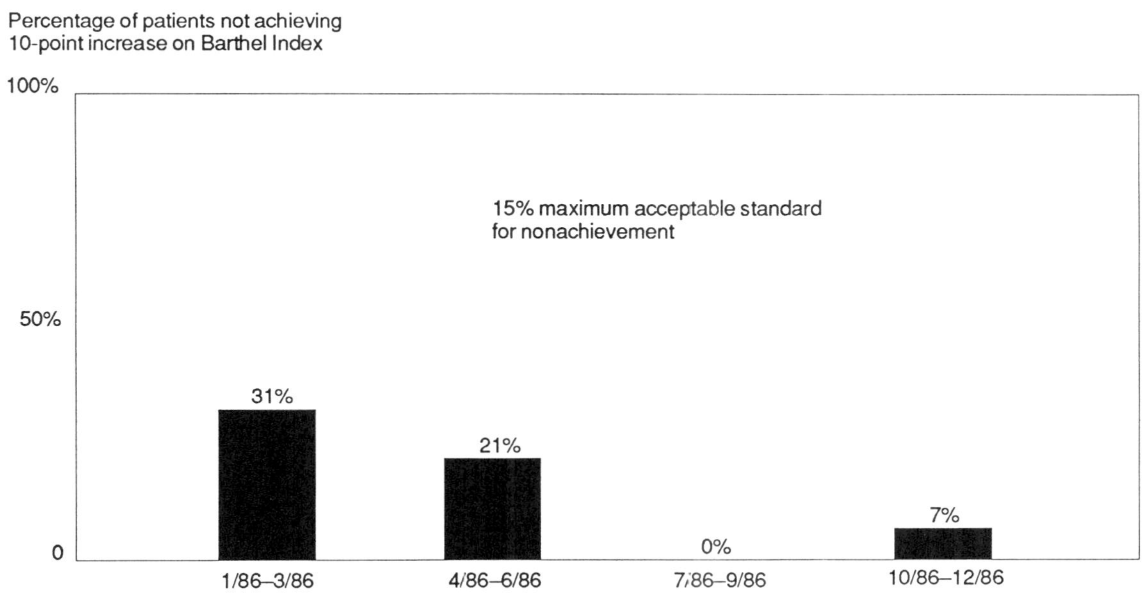

Table 7-b. The Barthel Index

	With Help		Independent
1. Feeding	5		10
2. Bed-chair transter	5	10	15
3. Grooming	0		5
4. On/off toilet	5		10
5. Bathing self	0		15
6. Walking on level surface	10		15
Wheelchair propulsion	0		5
7. Ambulation/stairs	5		10
8. Dressing/undressing	5		10
9. Bowel continence	5		10
10. Bladder control	5		10

0–20 = Totally dependent
21–61 = Severely dependent
62–90 = Moderately dependent
91–99 = Slightly dependent
100 = Independent

Table 7-c. A Hypothetical Example of Documentation for One Patient

CVA/Head Trauma Study Log

Barthel Index
0–20 = Totally dependent
21–61 = Severely dependent
62–90 = Moderately dependent
91–99 = Slightly dependent
100 = Independent

Name ______
Med. # ______
Age ______ Sex M
MEPS Date 9/14/85 Grade II
MEPS Date ______ Grade ______
OT PT Speech

Diagnosis (L) CVA c (R) hemiplegia

Date of Onset 8/30/85

	Initial Date	Discharge Date	Remarks
1. Feeding (10)	5	10	
2. Bed-chair transfer (15)	5	15	
3. Grooming (5)	0	5	
4. On/off toilet (10)	5	10	
5. Bathing self (5)	0	5	
6. Walking on level surface (15)	0	15	Safety depends on mental status.
Wheelchair propulsion (5)	0	5	
7. Ambulation/stairs (10)	0	10	
8. Dressing/undressing (10)	5	5	
9. Bowel continence (10)	10	10	
10. Bladder control (10)	10	10	
Barthel Index Total	40	100	
Cardiac tolerance to ADL			

Table 7-d. **A Hypothetical Example of a Log Recording Quality-Assurance Monitoring Data**

Rehabilitation Unit CVA and Head Trauma Functional Outcome

	Initial Score	Discharge Score	Initial Date	Discharge Date	Achievement	Nonachievement	Remarks
January–March 1986							
1.	55	75	2/21/86	3/8/86	x		
2.	10	50	12/7/85	1/12/86	x		
3.	15	40	1/25/86	2/12/86		x	
4.	60	85	2/13/86	3/10/86	x		Name, # missing
5.	60	90	2/25/86	3/21/86	x		
6.	55	65	1/2/86	1/31/86	x		
7.	70	95	---	---	x		No dates
8.	15	20	1/22/86	2/4/86		x	
9.	10	15	12/10/85	1/15/86		x	
10.	20	25	12/20/85	1/20/86		x	
11.	30	45	1/3/86	2/1/86	x		
12.	10	20	1/5/86	3/1/86	x		
13.	35	50	1/7/86	2/28/86	x		
14.							***31% Nonachievement***
15.							
April–June 1986							
1.	5	15	4/15/86	4/25/86	x		
2.	60	100	4/11/86	4/27/86	x		
3.	60	100	3/29/86	4/10/86	x		
4.	0	0	5/8/86	6/4/86		x	
5.	70	90	2/8/86	2/14/86	x		
6.	35	75	9/6/86	---	x		No D/C date
7.	45	70	6/17/86	6/3/86	x		
8.	50	95	---	---	x		No dates
9.	10	10	4/18/86	5/7/86		x	
10.	30	50	3/23/86	4/19/86		x	
11.	30	35	3/25/86	4/20/86	x		
12.	30	40	3/12/86	4/1/86	x		
13.	40	60	4/10/86	4/30/86	x		
14.	50	80	5/2/86	6/2/86	x		***21% Nonachievement***
15.							
July–September 1986							
1.	25	50	7/8/86	8/17/86	x		
2.	80	100	9/86	---	x		No D/C date
3.	0	45	6/11/86	8/15/86	x		
4.	0	20	7/9/86	8/6/86	x		No #
5.	25	40	---	---	x		No dates
6.	10	40	7/5/86	8/20/86	x		
7.	25	65	8/13/86	10/1/86	x		
8.	15	50	7/20/86	8/10/86	x		
9.	20	75	9/1/86	9/23/86	x		
10.	20	60	9/2/86	10/1/86	x		
11.							***0% Nonachievement***
12.							
13.							
14.							
15.							

Table 7-d (cont.)

	Initial Score	Dis-charge Score	Initial Date	Dis-charge Date	Achieve-ment	Non-achieve-ment	Remarks
October–December 1986							
1.	0	25	9/9/86	11/5/86	x		
2.	50	90	9/18/86	10/19/86	x		
3.	35	90	9/30/86	11/26/86	x		
4.	75	100	9/19/86	10/2/86	x		
5.	0	15	10/16/86	11/18/86	x		
6.	70	100	11/1/86	11/8/86	x		
7.	75	100	---	---	x		No dates
8.	30	30	11/26/86	12/15/86		x	
9.	60	85	11/11/86	12/13/86	x		
10.	70	85	9/29/86	10/12/86	x		
11.	20	65	10/2/86	10/31/86	x		
12.	10	25	9/30/86	11/6/86	x		
13.	15	30	11/2/86	12/15/86	x		
14.	35	80	10/1/86	12/1/86	x		
15.							***7% Nonachievement***
January–March 1987							
1.	10	40	2/14/87	4/5/87	x		
2.	45	80	1/27/87	2/7/87	x		
3.	40	75	11/20/86	1/17/87	x		
4.	30	70	---	---	x		No dates
5.	25	75	2/20/87	3/87	x		No #
6.	40	65	11/18/86	12/19/86	x		
7.							***0% Nonachievement***
8.							
9.							
10.							
11.							
12.							
13.							
14.							
15.							
April–June 1987							
1.	50	85	5/31/87	6/4/87	x		
2.	65	100	6/26/87	---	x		
3.	60	85	4/1/87	4/14/87	x		
4.	35	80	5/1/87	5/8/87	x		No #
5.	80	100	5/14/87	---	x		
6.	5	35	4/18/87		x		
7.	25	100	4/7/87	5/87	x		
8.	45	100	3/25/87	5/2/87	x		
9.	55	100	4/29/87	5/87	x		
10.	20	80	1/23/87	4/1/87	x		
11.	35	100	5/5/87	5/30/87	x		
12.							***0% Nonachievement***
13.							
14.							
15.							

Table 8. Hypothetical Monitor No. 2

Date	Indicator Stage 1	Criteria/Standard/ Measure Stage 2	Location of Data	Reviewer/ Date	Results/Date	Date Reported to Staff and Dept.Chair
July–September 1986	Completion of multidisciplinary rounds	90% of rehabilitation patients to be seen on a weekly basis during rounds[a]	OT Staff Room	Y. N. Secretary & A. K. QA Coordinator 10/3/86	274 Scheduled 208 Seen 24% Not seen	10/7/86 Rehab. Mgt. Staff
October–December 1986	Same as above	Same as above	Rounds log	Same as above 1/2/87	189 Scheduled 163 Seen 14% Not seen	1/7/87 Rehab. Mgt. Staff
January–March 1987	Same as above	Same as above	Same as above	Same as above 4/3/87	275 Scheduled 173 Seen 37% Not seen	3/13/87 Rehab. Mgt. Staff 4/7/87 Mgt. Staff
April–June 1987	Same as above	Same as above	Same as above	Same as above 7/1/87	267 Scheduled 238 Seen 11% Not seen	To be reported to Rehab. Mgt. Staff on 7/7/87

Note: Adapted from forms developed by Anne A. Kuntavanish, OTR, FAOTA, Rehabilitation Services Administrator, Greater Southeast Community Hospital, Washington, DC. Reprinted by permission. The example draws on actual quality assurance activities but has been altered for reasons of confidentiality. The monitoring system illustrated is basd on the five-stage problem-solving process of quality assurance described in Chapter 3.

[a]Whereas the goal is theoretically 100%, the consensus of professional opinion for this hypothetical study is that 10% of the patients may not be seen for valid reasons. These cases will be reviewed, however.

Table 8 (cont.)

Impact of Achieving Standard	Date	Recs. for Improvement Action Stage 3	Implem. Date & Improvement Action Stage 4	Reeval. Date/ Result Stage 5	Date Reported to Staff & Dept. Chair	Remarks
Timely care update may impact on LOS and maximum benefit in terms of functional outcome.	10/7/86	1. Prioritize patients on rounds list. 2. Evaluate rounds time slots.	10/8/86	1/3/87	Rehab. Mgt. Staff 1/7/87	Continue with present plan.
Same as above	1/7/87	Continue as above.				
Same as above	3/13/87	1. Patients who need change of order to be seen in the clinics when possible. 2. Give priority to weekly rounds.	3/18/87	4/3/87	To extend review through 6/87	
Same as above						

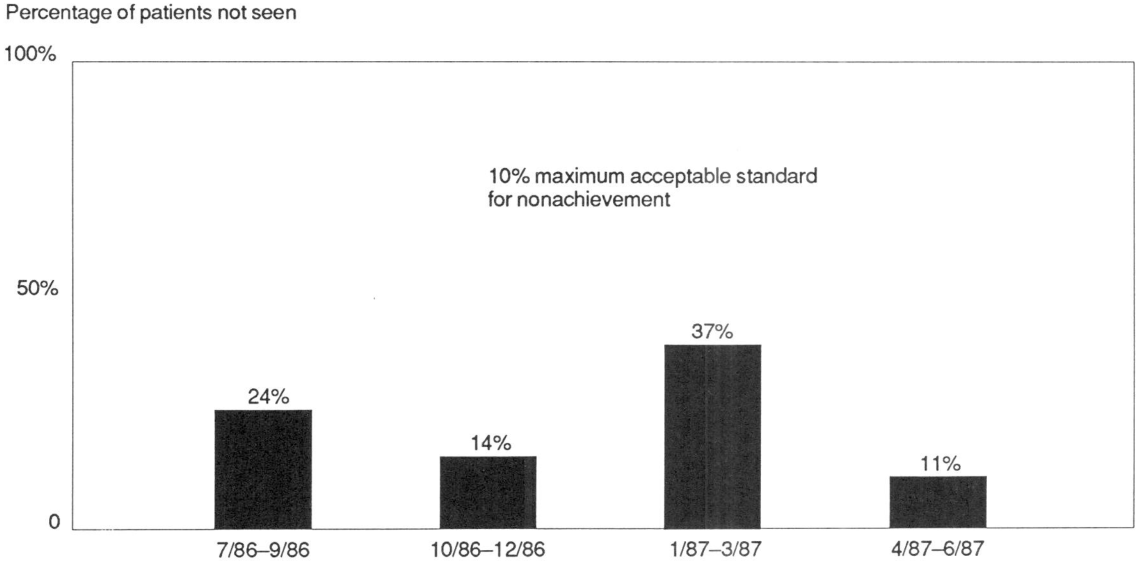

Index